I0828570

The Day the Lilacs Disappeared

Dr. Smriti Nayan

Illustrated by Dr. Smriti Nayan

With original sketches by Misha Bhapkar, age 8

Foreword by Dr. Martin Desrosiers

Illustrations by Dr. Smriti Nayan
Inspired by original sketches by Misha Bhapkar, age 8
Illustration Note: Some illustrations in this book were developed with the assistance of generative AI tools and were carefully reviewed, refined, and curated by the author to preserve the spirit of the original sketches while supporting the story's educational purpose, emotional tone, and visual consistency.

Foreword by Dr. Martin Desrosiers
Published in Canada by Lilac Press, 2026
ISBN 978-1-0673672-0-6
Printed by Amazon KDP (Print on Demand)
Display type set in Playfair Display. Body text set in Nunito.
Printed on sustainably sourced paper

Dedication

To my children, Misha and Milan, my two little stars, whose laughter and curiosity became Kushboo and Kamal, turning whispers into stories.

To my family, the roots and the wings, your steadfast love grounds me and lifts me through every endeavour.

And to my patients, the quiet gardeners of my days, who teach me endlessly and inspire me always; reminding me that even when a fragrance fades, its memory, like lilacs in spring, can bloom forever.

This story is as much yours as it is mine.

Foreword

We teach children to read eye charts and listen for sounds through headphones.
We celebrate vision and hearing as essential senses - measurable, testable, and routinely protected.

But the sense of smell, though equally vital to daily life and emotional well-being, remains largely invisible in medicine.
In Canada, smell testing is not yet part of standard health checks. Most clinics lack the tools or time to measure it. As a result, smell loss often goes unnoticed and untreated until it has quietly changed a person's quality of life.

As a clinician and researcher studying chronic rhinosinusitis, I see firsthand how profoundly smell loss can affect people. It blurs the taste of food, dulls memory, and steals the quiet joys that connect us to the world: a favourite meal, a loved one's scent, the lilacs in spring.

What we need now is awareness among clinicians, families, teachers, and children themselves.

Recognizing smell loss is the first step toward recognizing disease.

This book helps make that possible.
Through gentle storytelling and beautiful illustration, it introduces the importance of smell in language children can understand and emotions they can feel. It invites us as physicians, parents, and advocates to imagine a future where smell testing is as familiar as eye charts and hearing screens - where early recognition leads to timely, evidence-based care.

The Day the Lilacs Disappeared is more than a story - it is the beginning of a movement.

A reminder that even the most invisible senses deserve to be seen.

— Martin Desrosiers, MD, FRCSC
Professor, Rhinologist, Researcher
Montréal, Quebec

What Does "Kushboo" Mean?

In Hindi, Urdu and Bangla, the word Kushboo (pronounced Koosh-boo) means fragrance, a beautiful smell that stirs memories, feelings, and stories.

Fragrance is invisible, but powerful.
It reminds us of people we love, places we've been, and moments we never want to forget.
The scent of jasmine on a summer night.
The smell of your favourite stuffed toy or your mom's warm scarf.
The sweetness of lilacs in bloom.
Some smells are easy to describe.
Others? Not so much.
They make you feel happy, cozy, safe...
Even if you can't quite say why.
We often don't realize just how important our sense of smell is, until we lose it.

Smell helps keep us safe.
It warns us of smoke, spoiled food, or gas leaks.
It tells us when dinner's ready...or when something's not quite right.
That's what makes Kushboo such a special name.

This story is for everyone who has ever followed a scent straight into a memory and for those who are still learning to notice the invisible things that make life beautiful.

— Dr. Smriti Nayan MD, MSc, FRCSC

Glossary:
Kushboo - fragrance
Kamal - lotus flower in Hindi
Amma - Mother

Before Kushboo could see them...she could smell them.

A soft, purple sweetness floated through the air.
Gentle, joyful, and full of promise.

It was her favorite smell.
The one that came with spring.
The one that matched her name...like something too gentle to name.

Kushboo smiled and stepped outside.

She followed the fragrance, barefoot in the grass, past the swing, around the maple tree until she reached her lilac bush.

Underneath its branches, her little brother, Kamal, was already waiting.

"Smell is like a secret sense," Kushboo told Kamal.

"It finds things before your eyes do."
"Like pancakes before breakfast..."
"...or puddles after the rain."

She leaned in close.

"It even remembers things your heart forgets."

Kushboo's
Smell Journal
AMMA'S
ROSE OIL
WET EARTH
FIRST DAY
OF SPRING
JASMINE
AT NIGHT

Kushboo kept a smell journal.
She filled it with scribbles, stickers, and petals.

Each scent linked to a memory:

Amma's rose oil.

Wet earth on the first day of spring.

The jasmine by her window that only bloomed at night.

Kushboo woke up one morning and something felt wrong. The lilacs were still blooming, big and bright. But when Kushboo leaned in there was no smell.

She sniffed again. Still nothing. She sniffed the grass. The garden. Her own shirt. Nothing. Her nose wasn't stuffy and she didn't feel sick. The smell had simply slipped away.

At breakfast, she couldn't smell or taste the cinnamon toast.

At school, her glue stick smelled like...air.

At night, her pajamas just felt like fabric.

The world didn't look different. It didn't sound different.

But something invisible, something important, was gone.

"It's like my nose forgot how to feel," Kushboo whispered.

Kamal reached out and held her hand.
He didn't say anything. He didn't have to.

The next day, Kushboo and her mother went to see the doctor.

The doctor told Kushboo she likely had a bad cold. She was getting better but her sense of smell would take time to come back.

At school, Kushboo remembered how the nurse held up a big chart of letters for everyone to read.

She remembered the funny headphones with beeps, where you raised your hand if you heard them.

But for noses?
Nothing.

The doctor listened carefully.

“There’s no test for smell?” she asked the doctor.

The doctor shook her head. **“There are tests for smell,”** she said, **“but they aren’t easy for everyone to get. What matters most is how you feel.”**

Kushboo frowned. It felt unfair.
Why did it seem like smell was the forgotten sense.

She imagined a magical “sniff chart” with rows of lilacs, cinnamon buns, and chocolate chip cookies. Each one softer than the last until only the tiniest whisper was left.
But in real life, no such test existed. Not yet.

Kushboo tried to imagine the smell of jasmine. She tried to remember the way her mother's shawl used to make her feel safe.

She flipped through her smell journal and pressed her face into the pages. Nothing.

Her mother hugged her gently.

"Sometimes, our bodies need time," she said.

"And sometimes, they find new ways to remember their favourite things."

Kushboo began noticing things differently.

She watched how the lilacs swayed in the wind, how the sun painted the petals with gold.

She felt the tickle of grass on her knees, and the hush of the breeze as it moved past her cheek.

“I can still know things,” she told Kamal.

“Even if I can’t smell them.”

One quiet afternoon, Kushboo sat beside the lilacs again. She wasn't expecting anything. Just sitting. Just being. She closed her eyes and breathed. And there it was. Soft. Gentle. Purple. Only a whisper...but it was there.

FRAGRANCE

Smell wasn't just something Kushboo had.

It was something she noticed,
something she remembered,
something she would never take for granted again.

Because her name meant fragrance
and she knew, more than ever,
just how powerful a thing that was.

Fragrance lost,
fragrance found in every petal, sight, and sound.

Kushboo lost something
invisible and found
something unforgettable...

Author's Note

A Note for Parents and Educators: Why Smell Matters

Our sense of smell is vital for health and well-being, yet it is often overlooked.

Loss of smell is common. It can follow viral infections, head injuries, Alzheimer's or chronic conditions like chronic rhinosinusitis with nasal polyposis (CRSwNP). Smell can also be absent from birth.

It impacts daily life. Beyond food enjoyment, smell contributes to safety, emotional health, and memory.

It deserves attention. Too often, smell loss is dismissed as minor, but it can be life-altering and distressing.

Smell Testing for All

In Canada and globally, smell testing is rarely performed in routine care but it should be.

Routine smell testing:

Can support early diagnosis of medical conditions.
Guide treatment decisions (for example, in CRSwNP).
Validate patients' experiences, showing that smell loss is recognized and taken seriously.

By advocating for wider access to smell testing, we can help children and adults receive better care, raise awareness of this important sense, and remind everyone that smell is not optional, it is essential.

Smell Science (For Kids!)

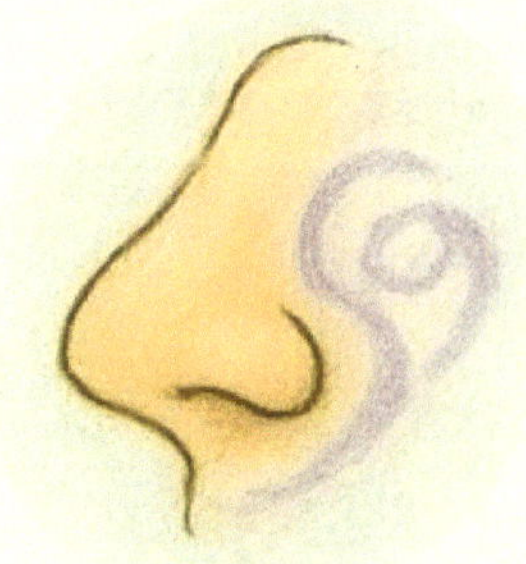

Most of us don't think much about our sense of smell - until it disappears.

Why Can Smell Disappear

After a cold or flu, smell can take some time to come back.

A head injury.

Some conditions like chronic rhinosinusitis with nasal polyps, block the nose and make smelling hard.

A few people are born without being able to smell.

Why Does Smell Matter?

It makes food taste delicious.

It warns us of danger (smoke, spoiled food, gas leaks)

It helps us remember special people, places, and moments.

Did you know? Some dogs can smell 100,000 times better than humans!

Acknowledgements

This book would not exist without the encouragement whose belief in the power of storytelling to advance patient care. His mentorship, generosity, and friendship have been among the greatest gifts of my career.

To the clinicians, researchers, educators, parents, and children who read early versions of this story and offered their time, expertise, and hearts - thank you. Your enthusiasm confirmed what I hoped: that smell deserves to be seen.

To my colleagues in otolaryngology, respirology and allergy, across Canada and the world, your dedication to your patients is the quiet force behind this work.

To my family, whose love makes everything possible.

And to every child who has ever stopped to notice something invisible, this book is for you.

About the Author

Dr. Smriti Nayan is an Otolaryngologist–Head & Neck Surgeon who helps children and adults breathe, smell, and feel better. She has seen the profound impact of smell loss on daily life, memories, and joy.

She wrote The Day the Lilacs Disappeared to help young readers understand just how precious the sense of smell truly is. The story was inspired by her patients, the lilacs that bloom each spring in Canada, and her own children, Misha and Milan.

The book was illustrated with the help of Misha, age 8, who contributed the first sketches before declaring her artistic duties complete.

When she isn't in the operating room or writing, Smriti can be found skiing with her family, exploring new places, or stopping to smell every flower she sees — especially lilacs.

This is her first children's book.

www.ingramcontent.com/pod-product-compliance
Lightning Source LLC
LaVergne TN
LVHW070224110826
845147LV00003B/635
* 9 7 8 1 0 6 7 3 6 7 2 0 6 *